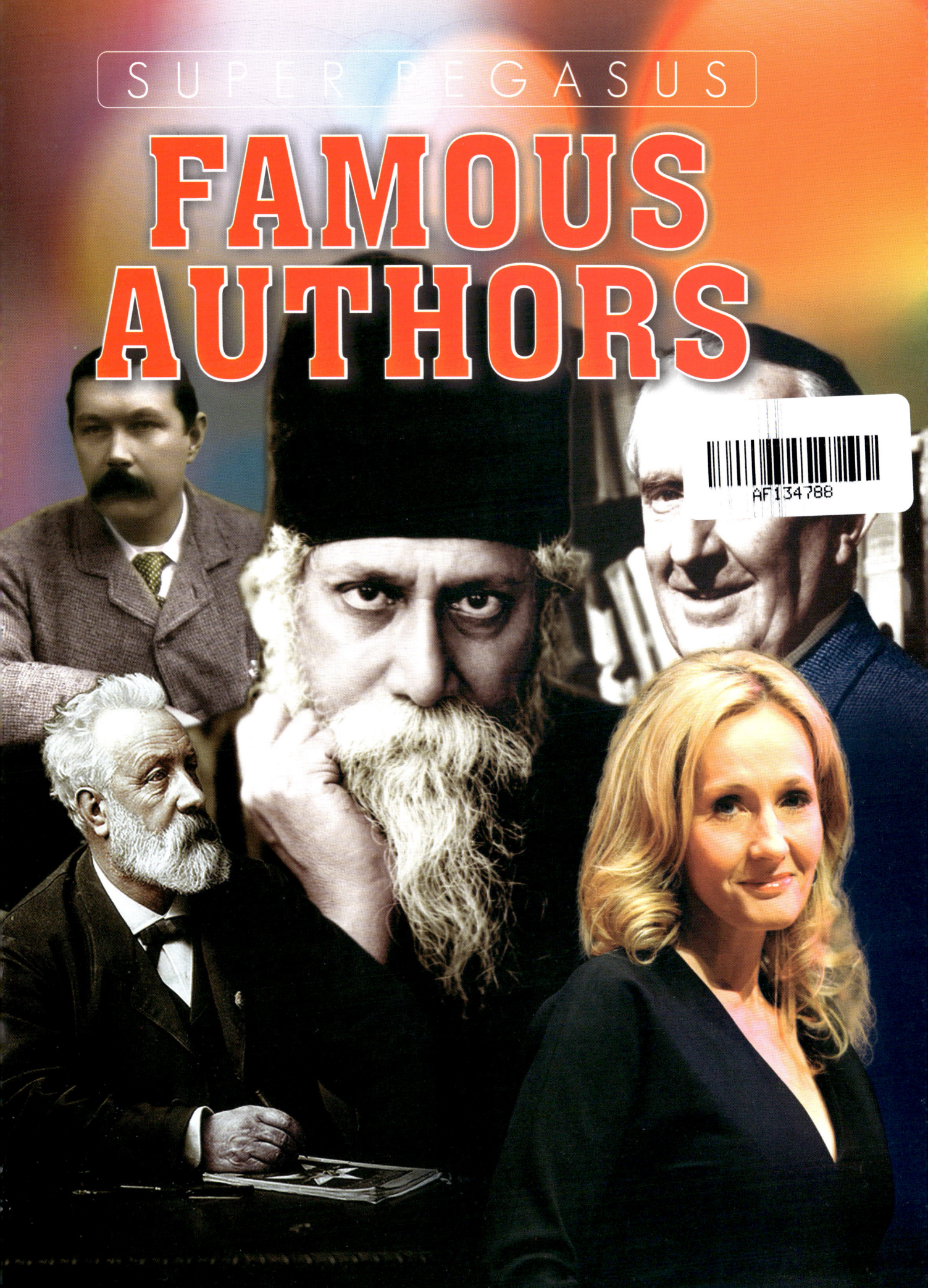

www.pegasusforkids.com

© **B. Jain Publishers (P) Ltd.** All rights reserved. No part of this book may be reproduced, stored in a retrieval system or transmitted, in any form or by any means, mechanical, photocopying, recording or otherwise, without any prior written permission of the publisher.

Published by Kuldeep Jain for B. Jain Publishers (P) Ltd., D-157, Sector 63, Noida - 201307, U.P

Printed in India

Image page nos. 3, 7, 8, 9, 11, 13, 14, 15, 30, 31, 32, 33, 37, 40, 41, 43, 44, 45, 48 © Copyright Getty Images India

Contents

4   **Alexandre Dumas**

6   Arthur Conan Doyle

10   **Charles Dickens**

14   J.K. Rowling

18   **J.R.R. Tolkien**

22   Jane Austen

26   **Jules Verne**

30   Leo Tolstoy

34   **Lewis Carroll**

36   Mark Twain

40   **Rabindranath Tagore**

44   William Shakespeare

ALEXANDRE DUMAS

Alexandre Dumas was born in Villers-Cotterêts, France, to Marie Louise Labouret and General Thomas-Alexandre Davy de la Pailleterie. His father was enlisted in the army of Napoleon and rose to the rank of General in the army.

Dumas attended Abbé Grégoire's school before dropping out to take a job assisting a local notary. As a child, he had heard stories of his father's bravery at the war front, which left an indelible impression on his wild imagination. Though they struggled to make ends meet, his father's reputation and aristocratic rank helped Dumas to advance in life. In 1822, Dumas moved to France, where he was introduced to the world of literature.

Writing Career

In 1822, Dumas moved to Paris and started working as a scribe for the ducd' Orléans. After the revolution, as the country started to industrialize and the press censorship ended, it proved a blessing for Dumas. He met noted playwrights and collaborated with them to make his debut on stage at Comédie Française. It was here that he put up noted plays like *Henry III and His Court* (1829), *The Tower of Nesle* (1832), *Kean* (1836), and *Antony* (first performed in 1831).

His plays, "fashioned according to the romantic movement," were a decided change from the Neo-Classical style that dominated Parisian stages at the time. He then began writing plays, both comedies and dramas. Dumas was a prolific writer of essays, short stories and novels. He also wrote plays and travelogues with equal zeal. As his work was popular and gained success, he tried his hand at writing novels. He achieved widespread success with the novels *The Count of Monte Cristo* and *The Three Musketeers*, which were initially published as serials. These novels made Dumas a household name in France, and a popular author in Europe. *The Count of Monte Cristo* (1844), first serialized in the weekly journal des *débats*, was also a huge literary and financial success for Dumas. His novels were translated in different languages during this time.

With the money he earned from publishing his novels, Dumas purchased land and built the Château de Monte Cristo in Port Marly, Yvelines, France. This home was intended to be a sanctuary for the author. After a short but terrifying bout of cholera during the epidemic of 1832, Dumas travelled throughout Europe to recover. During these trips, he kept detailed records of his travels, which were later published between 1834 and 1860.

He spent much of his time writing at his home along with organizing lavish gatherings for his friends. Soon, he was in debt and had to sell the property. In order to further evade the debtors, he went to Belgium in 1851, and later to Russia in a self-imposed exile. During this time, he continued to write and publish plays, essays and stories including travelogues.

Personal Life

Dumas had a son, also named Alexandre, with Marie Laure Catherine Labay. His son followed in his father's literary footsteps. In 1840, Dumas married actress Ida Ferrier.

Death and Legacy

Dumas died on December 5, 1870, at his son's home in Puys, France. He was buried in the cemetery of Villers-Cotterêts. In 2002, his body was moved to the Panthéon in Paris, where Dumas rests among other French literary greats as Émile Zola, Victor Hugo and Jean-Jacques Rousseau. To this day, he remains one of the most famous and among the most read French authors.

Fast Facts

Dumas was one of the most notable French authors in the world. His works have been translated in more than 100 languages.

ARTHUR CONAN DOYLE

Arthur Conan Doyle was born into an affluent, strict Irish-Catholic family in Edinburgh, Scotland. His family was well respected in the art world. His father, however, had few accomplishments to speak of. Doyle's mother, Mary, on the other hand, was a lively and well-educated woman who loved to read. Due to his father's weakness for alcohol, the family dispersed in 1864 but came together again in 1867. His mother told her young son outlandish stories to entertain them. Her great enthusiasm and animation while spinning wild tales sparked young Doyle's imagination.

As a 9 year old, Doyle bid a tearful adieu to his parents and came to England to study at the Jesuit preparatory school Hodder Place. He then went on to study at Stonyhurst College for the next five years. For Doyle, the boarding school experience was nothing less than brutal. He later wrote that he was often bullied by his classmates. Also, the school punished its students harshly. During these years, Doyle found comfort in his natural ability for storytelling. In no time, he had an audience for his stories among the younger students.

Medical Education and Career

Doyle graduated from Stonyhurst College in 1876 and his parents expected him to pursue art. He, however, wanted to study for a medical degree at the University of Edinburgh, which left his family surprised. Around this time, Doyle also started writing short stories. At medical school, Doyle met his mentor, Professor Dr Joseph Bell, whose keen powers of observation would later inspire Doyle to create his famed fictional detective character, Sherlock Holmes. At the University, he studied along with future fellow authors James Barrie and Robert Louis Stevenson. Among the first stories that Doyle had written during this time were *The Mystery of Sasassa Valley* and *The American Tale*.

During Doyle's third year of medical school, he took a ship surgeon's post on a whaling ship that was bound for the Arctic Circle. This voyage awakened his sense of adventure. In 1880, Doyle returned to medical school. He now became increasingly influenced by spiritualism and psychic religion, a belief system that he would later attempt to spread through a series of his written works. A year later, Doyle received his degree in medicine. In the same year, he left the Catholic faith and turned a spiritualist. He first started practicing as a doctor on board the steamship Mayumba. After a while, Doyle settled in Plymouth, England. In 1882, he joined former classmate George Turnavine Budd as his partner at a medical practice in Plymouth. He soon went independent but as his practice did not find him success, he began writing fiction stories in his clinic. Around 1890, he studied ophthalmology in Vienna but again his practice as an ophthalmologist proved to be unsuccessful. All this while, he continued to write. In time, Doyle would give up medicine altogether to become a full-time writer.

Personal Life

In 1885, while still struggling as a writer, Doyle met Louisa Hawkins and soon got married to her. The couple bore two children—a daughter and a son. In 1893, Louisa was diagnosed with tuberculosis. While she was ailing, Doyle became close to a young woman, Jean Leckie. Louisa died in 1906 and a year later, Doyle married Jean.

Writing Career

In 1886, while struggling as a writer, Doyle started writing the mystery novel *A Tangled Skein*. Two years later, he renamed the work, *A Study in Scarlet*, and it was published in Beeton's *Christmas Annual*. It was the first novel

to introduce the world-famous characters Detective Sherlock Holmes and his assistant, Dr Watson, and the one which finally earned Doyle the fame he was yearning for. From here on, there was no looking back for Doyle, and he went on to write 60 more stories around these two central characters.

Sherlock Holmes was Doyle's most famous creation but his attitude towards Holmes was uncertain. Around 1891, he wanted to get rid of Holmes so that he could write about other matters. Then, in order to discourage the demand for Sherlock Holmes stories, he raised his price so that he would not be bothered. However, even a price hike did not deter publishers from pursuing him for more Sherlock Holmes stories. In December 1893, to dedicate more of his time to his historical novels, Doyle had Holmes and Professor Moriarty plunge to their deaths together down the Reichenbach Falls in the story, *The Final Problem*. The public raised a huge outcry and he had to bring back Holmes in 1901 in the novel *The Hound of the Baskervilles*. In 1903, Doyle published his first Holmes short story in 10 years, *The Adventure of the Empty House*. He went on to publish stories on Sherlock Holmes till 1927. Even to this day, Holmes remains Doyle's most famous character.

Doyle continued to actively participate in the Spiritualist Movement and wrote three autobiographies between 1887 and 1916. These include *Beyond the City* (1893), *The Stark Munro Letters* (1895), and *A Duet with an Occasional Chorus* (1899). Since he had had success as a writer, he gave up practicing medicine completely. Throughout this period, he additionally produced a handful of historical novels including one about the Napoleonic Era called *The Great Shadow* in 1892 and his most famous historical novel, *Rodney Stone*, in 1896.

The prolific author also composed four of his most popular Sherlock Holmes books during the 1890s and early 1900s: *The Sign of the Four, The Adventures of Sherlock Holmes, The Memoirs of Sherlock Holmes* and *The Hound of Baskervilles*. Doyle also attempted to spread Spiritualism amid his readership through many of his written works including *The New Revolution, The Vital Message, The Wanderings of a Spiritualist* and *History of Spiritualism*. In 1928, Doyle's final 12 stories about Sherlock Holmes were published in a compilation, *The Casebook of Sherlock Holmes*.

Death

In his later years, Doyle complained of chest pain but he stubbornly ignored them. He even went on a spiritualism tour to the Netherlands in 1929. On his return, he suffered from chest pains so severe that he had to be carried to shore, so he could recover. But he remained bedridden at his home in Crowborough, England. Rising one last time on July 7, 1930, Doyle collapsed and died in his garden as he clutched his heart with one hand and held a flower in the other.

Fast Facts

Doyle was a talented cricketer. Although his cricket career never brought him much fame, he is said to have named Sherlock after a cricketer who played for Northampton.

CHARLES DICKENS

Famed British author Charles Dickens was born in Portsmouth, on the southern coast of England. He was the second of his eight siblings. His father, John Dickens, was a naval clerk who dreamed of striking it rich. His mother, Elizabeth Barrow, aspired to be a teacher and school director. Despite his parents' best efforts, the family remained poor. The family however was a happy one, at least during Dickens' growing-up years. In 1816, the family moved to Chatham, Kent, where the young Dickens and his siblings spent some memorable days in the countryside.

In 1822, the Dickens family moved to a poor neighbourhood in London. By now, the family was struggling to make ends meet. His father had also landed himself in deep debt. When he was unable to pay it, he was sent to prison in 1824. Dickens was 12 years old at that time.

After his father's imprisonment, young Dickens was forced to leave school to work at a boot-blacking factory alongside the River Thames. At the rundown, rodent-ridden factory, Dickens earned six shillings a week labeling pots of 'blacking'—a substance used to clean fireplaces. Dickens was not much in favour of the work and in his later years, he described the experience as the moment when his youthful innocence was 'gone for good'. The experience of these young years became a recurring theme in his later years as a writer.

Much to his relief, Dickens returned to school when his father received a family inheritance, which the former used to pay off his debts. When Dickens was 15, once more his education was stopped. In 1827, he had to drop out of school and work as an office boy to add to his family's income. This opportunity however turned out to be the base to launch his career as a writer.

A year later, Dickens began freelance reporting at the law courts of London. Soon, he was reporting for two major London newspapers. In 1833, he began submitting sketches drawn by him to various magazines and newspapers under the pseudonym 'Boz'. In 1836, his clippings were published in his first book, *Sketches by Boz*. It was also around this time that Dickens met Catherine Hogarth, who he later married.

Early Writing

In the same year that *Sketches by Boz* was released, Dickens started publishing *The Posthumous Papers of the Pickwick Club*. His series of sketches, originally written as captions for artist Robert Seymour's humourous sports-themed illustrations, took the form of monthly serial installments. *The Posthumous Papers of the Pickwick Club* was highly popular among the readers giving Dickens his first taste of major success.

Around this time, Dickens had also become publisher of a magazine called *Bentley's Miscellany*. It was here that he published his first novel, *Oliver Twist*, which followed the life of an orphan, who was forced to make his living while living on the streets. The story was inspired by Dickens' experiences as a child when he was forced to work. *Oliver Twist* was also printed in magazines, while in its novel form it received much acclaim both in England and America.

Over the next few years, Dickens struggled to match the success of *Oliver Twist*. From 1838 to 1841, he published *The Life and Adventures of Nicholas Nickleby*, *The Old Curiosity Shop* and *Barnaby Rudge*. However, these books failed to match the brilliance of *Oliver Twist*.

In 1842, Dickens and his wife, Kate, went to the United States for a five-month long lecture tour. After their return, Dickens penned *American Notes for General Circulation*, a sarcastic travelogue criticizing American culture and materialism.

Over the next few years, Dickens published two Christmas stories, one of them being the now famous Christmas classic, *A Christmas Carol*.

Fame

During his first U.S. tour, in 1842, Dickens designated himself as what many have deemed the first modern celebrity. He spoke of his opposition to slavery and expressed his support for additional reform. His lectures were well received and people attended them in great numbers.

Although Dickens enjoyed the attention at first, he eventually realized that the constant attention was disrupting his private life. He was also annoyed by the various crude habits of the Americans. On his second tour to America, he tried to understand the American ways and culture. By the time of his return, Dickens had become so famous that people recognized him all over London as he strolled around the city. During these walks, he made observations about everyday life that would inspire his future works.

Later Years

From 1845 till the next two years, Dickens published in installments his next novel, *Dealings with the Firm of Dombey and Son*. In this novel, he wrote about how business tactics affect a family's personal finances. The novel had a darker tone and it also set the tone for his later works.

From 1849 to 1850, Dickens worked on *David Copperfield*, the first work of its kind. Until then, there was no single work that followed a character through his everyday life. While writing this particular novel, Dickens used instances from his own childhood when he worked as a journalist. *David Copperfield* was his personal favourite although it is not considered Dickens' best work.

During the 1850s, Dickens separated from his wife of many years and later had a relationship with a young actress. Even his novels took on a dark tone and his stories presented a gloomy worldview. In *Bleak House*, published in installments from 1852 to 1853, he deals with the hypocrisy of British society. *Hard Times*, which was published in 1854, took place in an industrial town at the peak of the economic expansion. *Little Dorrit* is also among Dickens dark novels. In this fiction, Dickens shows the conflict between human values and the world's brutality.

Marking a shift from his 'dark novel' period, Dickens published *A Tale of Two Cities* in 1859, which has its setting at the time of the French Revolution. His next novel, *Great Expectations* (1860–1861), considered his greatest masterpiece, focused on the moral development of its protagonist Pip.

Death

In 1865, Dickens was involved in a train accident, from which he never fully recovered. He continued to tour despite his failing health. He had a stroke on June 9, 1870, and died in Kent at his family home.

Fast Facts

Most of the characters in Dickens' novels are based on people he met and got acquainted with.

J.K. ROWLING

J.K. Rowling is the famous British author of the worldwide popular *Harry Potter* series. Rowling's journey has literally been from rags to riches. Today, Rowling and Harry Potter have become household names.

Growing Up Years

Rowling was born to Peter James Rowling, a Rolls-Royce aircraft engineer, and Anne Rowling, a science technician, in Yate, Gloucestershire, England. Rowling's sister Dianne was born when Rowling was roughly two years old. When Rowling was four, her family moved to Winterbourne. She studied at St. Michael's Primary School. It is believed that drew inspiration from the headmaster at her school, Alfred Dunn, for the *Harry Potter* series.

As a child, Rowling often wrote fantasy stories, which she read to her sister. When Rowling was nine years old, she started attending Church Cottage in Gloucestershire. She completed her secondary education at Wyedean School and College. When Rowling was a teenager, her great-aunt gave her a copy of Jessica Mitford's autobiography, *Hons and Rebels*. In no time, Mitford captivated Rowling's thought process and she read all of her books. Rowling has often quoted about being unhappy during her teenage years. Her stay at home was complicated by her mother's illness and she had a strained relationship with her father. She has also said that she based the character of Hermione Granger on herself when she was 11. Sean Harris, her best friend in the Upper Sixth, owned a turquoise Ford Anglia. This car inspired Rowling for a flying version of the same, which appeared in the second book of the *Harry Potter* series, *Harry Potter and the Chamber of Secrets*.

Early Writing Career

In 1982, Rowling took the entrance exams for Oxford University but was refused admission. She then read for a BA in French and Classics at the University of Exeter. After a year of study in Paris, Rowling graduated from Exeter in 1986 and moved to London to work as a researcher and bilingual secretary for Amnesty International. In 1988, Rowling wrote a short essay about her time studying classics entitled *What Was the Name of that Nymph Again?* It was later published in the University of Exeter's journal *Pegasus*.

After a while, she moved to Manchester and began working at the Chamber of Commerce. In 1990, during a four-hour delayed train trip from Manchester to London, Rowling conceived the idea of Harry Potter. Her mind was suddenly flooded with ideas about a boy who attended a school of magic. With no pen with her, she kept thinking about the story and immediately sat down to write it as soon as she reached home. In the same year, her mother passed away. Greatly affected by her mother's death, she rewrote the details about Harry's loss for now she knew how it felt.

Rowling moved to Porto in northern Portugal in the 1990s, where she taught English. She later met and married a Portuguese television journalist in October 1992 and gave birth to a daughter in 1993. However, the marriage lasted only for a year and she returned with her infant daughter to Edinburgh to live with her sister. By then, Rowling had three completed chapters of Harry Potter in her suitcase.

During that time, Rowling felt herself a failure with no job and a child who was dependent on her. It was a difficult time for her and she went into depression. In 1994, she divorced her husband. The following year, she began a teacher training

course at the Moray House School of Education, Edinburgh University. She, however, continued to live on state benefits as she had declared herself poor. In order to complete her books, she wrote in many cafés, especially Nicolson's Café and the Elephant House; wherever she could get Jessica, her daughter, to fall asleep.

Breakthrough and Success

In 1995, Rowling finished her manuscript for *Harry Potter and the Philosopher's Stone*. Upon the enthusiastic response of Bryony Evens, a reader who had read the book's first three chapters, Christopher Little Literary Agents (a literary agents firm) agreed to represent Rowling to the publishers. The book was submitted to twelve publishers but everyone rejected her story. Then, editor Barry Cunningham of Bloomsbury, a publishing house in London, decided to publish her book. The decision was taken after Alice Newton, the eight-year-old daughter of Bloomsbury's chairman, who had read the first chapter, at once demanded to read the next. Rowling, however, was told that she should not raise her hopes high. Soon after, in 1997, Rowling received £ 8,000 grant from the Scottish Arts Council to enable her to continue writing.

In June 1997, Bloomsbury published *Philosopher's Stone* with an initial print run of 1,000 copies, 500 of which were distributed to libraries. Five months later, the book won its first award, a Nestlé Smarties Book Prize followed by more prizes. In early 1998, Scholastic Inc, won the rights to publish her novel in the United States. In October 1998, Scholastic published her book in the US under the title of *Harry Potter and the Sorcerer's Stone*.

In no time, the book was a huge success not only among children but also among adults. For Rowling, there was no looking back and she published a series of seven Harry Potter books. In July 1998, a sequel was published, titled Harry Potter and the Chamber of Secrets. The third book in the series, *Harry Potter and the Prisoner of Azkaban*, was published in December 1999. The fourth book, *Harry Potter and the Goblet of Fire* was released simultaneously in the UK and the US, in July 2000. This book broke all sales records for any book on the day of its release. *Harry Potter and the Order of the Phoenix*, the fifth in the series, was released three years later followed by *Harry Potter and the Half-Blood Prince* in July 2005. The seventh and the penultimate one, *Harry Potter and the Deathly Hallows*, came out in July 2007.

In addition to these books, Rowling has also written two small volumes, which appear as the titles of Harry's school books within the novels—*Fantastic Beasts and Where to Find Them* and *Quidditch Through the Ages*. Later, in 2008, she also penned down *The Tales of Beedle the Bard*.

Rowling has won several awards and honorary degrees for her work. Today, she also supports a number of charitable causes through the means of her charitable trust Volant. She has also founded a charity named Lumos, which is working to change the lives of disadvantaged children.

In 2012, Rowling published her first novel for adults, *The Casual Vacancy*. It was published in 44 languages. Among other notable works, Rowling has received much praise for *The Cuckoo's Calling* (2013), her first crime novel under the pseudonym Robert Galbraith, and its sequels, *The Silkworm and Career of Evil*.

Rowling continues to write books for children and for adults alike. Currently, Rowling lives in Edinburgh with her husband and three children.

Fast Facts

When her first Harry Potter novel was going to print, the publisher asked her to use her initials rather than her full name to eliminate any sort of biasness for female writers.

J.R.R. TOLKIEN

John Ronald Reuel Tolkien was born in Bloemfontein, South Africa to Arthur Tolkien and Mabel Suffield Tolkien. As a child, he was bitten by a large baboon spider in the garden and it is often assumed that this event echoes in his stories.

When he was three, he went to England with his mother and brother on a long visit. Back home, his father contracted rheumatic fever and he died before his family could join him. Unable to understand how to make a living for her family, Tolkien's mother moved in with her parents to Birmingham. Soon after, in 1896, they moved to Sarehole, a village in Worcestershire. The scenic beauty of the place later inspired several scenes in his books. Interestingly, his aunt Jane's farm, Bag End, finds mention in several of his works.

Tolkien's mother home-schooled her two children. Ronald, as he was known in the family, was a keen pupil. His mother taught him botany and awakened in him the ability to enjoy the world of plants. While young, Tolkien liked to draw landscapes and trees. But it was the ability to learn languages which fascinated Tolkien. At the tender age of four, he could read and write fluently, and learned Latin in the younger years of his life. Looking at his fascination with languages, his mother encouraged him to read books. He disliked *Treasure Island* and *The Pied Piper*, and thought that Alice's Adventures in Wonderland was "amusing but disturbing". Stories about Red Indians and the fairy tales of Andrew Lang inspired him and influenced his future writings.

When their mother died in 1904, the Tolkien brothers were sent to live with a relative and in boarding homes while a Catholic priest in Birmingham became their guardian. Father Francis, as Tolkien called him, taught him to be generous, to forgive and to do charity.

After his mother's death, Tolkien grew up in Edgbaston, Birmingham and attended King Edward's School and later St. Philip's School. In 1903, he won a Foundation Scholarship and returned to King Edward's. While a pupil there, Tolkien was one of the cadets from the school's Officers Training Corps V and was posted outside the Buckingham Palace. The incidents that took place during this time too inspired his works.

In his early teens, Tolkien had his first encounter with a constructed language, Animalic, which was invented by his cousins Mary and Marjorie Incledon. At that time, he was studying Latin and Anglo-Saxon. In no time, Tolkien along with his cousins had developed a more complex language called Nevbosh. He further created a new language on his own called Naffarin.

In 1911, Tolkien went on a summer holiday to Switzerland, a trip that he recollected vividly in a 1968 letter. In it, he mentioned that Bilbo's journey across the Misty Mountains was based on his adventures during this trip. In October 1911, he started attending Exeter College in Oxford, first studying Classics but later switching to a course on English language and literature.

Courtship and Marriage

Tolkien was 16 when he met Edith Mary Bratt, who was three years his senior. Around this time, he and his brother Hilary were living in a boarding house. His guardian, Father Morgan, viewed Edith as the reason for Tolkien's having "muffed" his exams and thought it unfortunate that his surrogate son was romantically involved with an older, Protestant woman. He therefore restricted him from meeting, talking or writing to her till he was 21 years of age. Tolkien followed the prohibition though it was a difficult task. Later, at 21, he was engaged to Edith.

After their engagement, Edith announced that she was converting to Catholicism

at Tolkien's insistence. Her decision was opposed but she went ahead. They were later married in March 1916. In his 1941 letter to his son Michael, Tolkien admired his wife for her willingness to marry a man with no job, little money and no prospects. Tolkien joined World War I as a second Lieutenant in 1916 and was transported to France.

Career as a Scholar and Writer

Continuing his linguistic studies, Tolkien joined the faculty of the University of Leeds in 1920 after the war and a few years later, he became a professor at Oxford University. While there he started a writing group called The Inklings, which counted among its members C.S. Lewis and Owen Barfield. It was also at Oxford, while grading a paper, that he spontaneously wrote a short line about "a hobbit."

The award-winning fantasy novel *The Hobbit*, about the small, fur-footed Bilbo Baggins and his adventures, was published in 1937. The book was considered a children's book though Tolkien had not intended it to be one. He also drew about 100 illustrations for the story. Over the years, while working on scholarly publications, Tolkien developed the work that would become his masterpiece—*The Lord of the Rings*. The series was partially inspired by European myths and he had its own maps, languages and stories for the series.

Tolkien released part one of the series, *The Fellowship of the Ring*, in 1954; *The Two Towers* and *The Return of the King* followed in 1955, winding up the trilogy. The books gave readers a rich literary trove populated by elves, goblins, talking trees and all kinds of fantastic creatures. While *The Lord of the Rings* had its share of critics, many reviewers and general readers loved the world created by Tolkien and elevated the books to the rank of bestsellers.

Famous Works

The Hobbit

Tolkien never expected his stories to gain such widespread popularity but by sheer accident a book called *The Hobbit*, which he had written for his own children, grabbed the attention of Susan Dagnall, an employee of the London publishing firm George Allen & Unwin. She persuaded Tolkien to submit the book for publication. The book became so popular that soon the publishers asked Tolkien to write a sequel to it.

The Lord of the Rings

At the request for a sequel, Tolkien began to write what became his most famous work—*The Lord of the Rings*. It was originally published as three books. He spent years writing the primary narrative and the appendices for the book. Both *The Hobbit* and *The Lord of the Rings* are set against the background of *The Silmarillion*, though the events of the books happen long after the time depicted in *The Silmarillion*. Though *The Lord of the Rings* is a sequel to *The Hobbit*, it is darker, more serious and addressed to an older audience. With the success of *The Lord of the Rings*, the fantasy genre, devised by Tolkien, grew.

The Lord of the Rings continues to captivate readers and ranks as one of the most popular works of fiction of the 20th century. Tolkien retired from professorial duties in 1959, going on to publish an essay and poetry collection, *Tree and Leaf*, and the fantasy tale *Smith of Wootton Major*. His wife Edith died in 1971 and Tolkien followed her in September 1973. He is survived by their four children.

Legacy

The Hobbit and *The Lord of the Rings* are grouped among the most popular books in the world. *The Lord of the Rings* trilogy and *The Hobbit* have also been adapted into award-winning films. Tolkien's son Christopher has edited several works that weren't completed at the time of his father's death, including The Silmarillion and *The Children of Húrin*, which were published posthumously.

Fast Facts

Owing to his connection with fictional history, fantasy writing, and constructed languages, Tolkien came to be known as the 'father of modern fantasy literature'.

JANE AUSTEN

Jane Austen, considered one of the greatest English writers, remained unknown during her lifetime though her works were well received. Today, most of her novels have become literary classics and are appreciated worldwide. Jane's parents, George Austen and his wife Cassandra, were members of substantial gentry families. While George descended from a family of woollen manufacturers, Cassandra belonged to the prominent Leigh family. From 1765 until 1801, George served as the rector of the Anglican parishes at Steventon, Hampshire. From 1773 until 1796, he supplemented this income by farming and by teaching three or four boys who stayed at his home.

Jane's immediate family was large, with six brothers and one sister, Cassandra who, like Jane, remained unmarried. Cassandra was Jane's closest friend and confidante.

Of her brothers, Jane was closest to Henry, who was also his sister's literary agent. He gave Jane a vast view of the social world at that time, as he had many contacts and several friends. Charles and Frank, her brothers, both served in the navy and rose to the rank of admiral.

Early Life and Education

When Jane was born, she was nursed by her mother for a few months following which she was put under the care of Elizabeth Littlewood, one of her neighbours. Elizabeth raised Jane for over a year. In 1783, according to family tradition, Jane and Cassandra were sent to Oxford for further education. A year later, they moved to Southampton, where both the girls caught typhus. Jane was subsequently educated at home, until leaving for boarding school with her sister Cassandra early in 1785. By December 1786, Jane and Cassandra had returned home as their parents could not afford to send both their daughters to school. Jane now stayed at home, spent most of her time in reading books, and took to writing.

Jane acquired the remainder of her education by reading books, guided by her father and her brothers, James and Henry. She apparently had unfettered access to her father's library. Her father was also tolerant of Jane's sometimes risqué experiments with writing. Private theatricals were also a part of Jane's education. In her younger days, her family and some of their closest friends staged plays for amusement. Most of these plays were comedies, the possible source of Jane's wit and humour.

Perhaps as early as 1787, Jane began to write poems, stories and plays for her family's amusement. She later compiled 'fair copies' of 29 of these early works into three bound notebooks, now referred to as the *Juvenilia*. Jane continued to work on these pieces as late as 1809–1811, and later on additions to them were made by her niece and nephew. Among these works are a satirical novel in letters titled *Love and Friendship* and *The History of England*, a parody of historical writings.

Adulthood

As Jane grew into adulthood, she continued to live at her parents' home, carrying out those activities normal for women of her age and social standing. Jane was particularly proud of her accomplishments as a seamstress. She read novels and often read her works to her family in the evenings.

In 1793, she began and then abandoned a short comic play, later entitled *Sir Charles Grandison or the Happy Man*, which she completed around 1800. This was a short parody of various school textbook abridgments of Jane's favourite contemporary novel, *The History of Sir Charles Grandison* (1753), by Samuel

Richardson. After finishing *Love and Friendship*, Jane decided to become a professional writer. She then began to write longer, sophisticated works, including a short epistolary novel titled *Lady Susan*.

Famous Works

Sense and Sensibility

Jane's first major novel was *Sense and Sensibility*, which revolved around the characters of two sisters. The first draft of the novel was written in 1795, and titled *Elinor and Marianne*. In 1797, Jane rewrote the novel and titled it *Sense and Sensibility*. It was published in 1811. The novel is about the temperaments of two sisters, one governed by reason and the other by her feelings. The novel favours the need for enlarged thought and feelings in the wake of circumstances and human emotions.

Pride and Prejudice

In 1796, Austen wrote the novel *First Impressions*. It later became known as *Pride and Prejudice* and was published in 1813. The novel went on to become her most notable work and today, it is considered among the greatest works ever written.

The resolution of the main plot with the marriage of the two opposite characters represents a reconciliation of conflicting moral extremes.

Mansfield Park

In 1811, Jane began to write *Mansfield Park*, which was published in 1814. It presents a conservative view of ethics, politics and religion. The story revolves around the central heroine who lives her life with upright character and dignity, and is triumphant in the end.

Emma

Emma, published in 1816, is the story of a girl of high intelligence and vivid imagination, who is also marked by egotism and a desire to dominate the lives of others. The events of the novel do change the main protagonist. *Emma* is considered by many critics as Jane's most brilliant work.

Persuasion

Persuasion, begun in 1815 and published posthumously in 1818, was Jane's last complete novel. The novel is perhaps most directly expressive of her feelings about her own life. Her satirical treatment of social pretensions and worldly motives is perhaps at its best in this novel. However, the dominant tone of *Persuasion* is not satirical but romantic. This book is perhaps Jane's most uncomplicated love story.

Later Life

After her father's death in 1805, the family went through extreme financial crisis. Jane, her mother and Cassandra started moving between homes of family members and rented flats. It was only in 1809 that they were able to settle into a stable living situation at Jane's brother Edward's cottage in Chawton.

Now in her 30s, Jane started to publish her works using a pseudonym. From 1811 to 1816, she got published *Sense and Sensibility*, *Pride and Prejudice*, *Mansfield Park* and *Emma*.

Death and Legacy

In 1816, at the age of 41, Jane began to suffer from ill health. She however continued to write at a normal pace. She even edited her older works and started working on a new novel called *The Brothers*, which would be published after her death as *Sanditon*. At one point Jane's condition deteriorated to such an extent that she was unable to write. She died on July 18, 1817, in Winchester, England, and was buried in the Winchester Cathedral.

Jane received much accolade for her works while she was alive, with her first three novels garnering critical attention and increasing her finances. She, however, was revealed as the author of the books by her brother Henry after her death. Today, Jane is considered one of the greatest writers in English history, both by academics and the general public. Her transformation from a little known to an internationally

renowned author started in the 1920s, when academics and scholars began to recognize her works as masterpieces. In no time the popularity of her works increased tremendously and they were adapted in films as well as television series.

Fast Facts

All of Jane Austen's work was published anonymously while she was alive.

JULES VERNE

Jules Verne was born in Nantes, France, a busy maritime port city. Seeing the ships arriving and departing at the port fuelled Verne's imagination as a child with stories of adventure. His father Pierre Verne was an attorney while his mother, Sophie Allote de la Fuÿe, belonged to a family of ship-owners and navigators. He was the eldest child in his family with a younger brother and three sisters.

In 1834, at the age of six, Verne attended a boarding school in Nantes followed by a catholic school. He quickly distinguished himself in recitation from memory, geography, Greek, Latin and singing.

Legend has it that in 1839, at the age of 11, Verne secretly procured a spot as cabin boy on the three-mast ship Coralie, with the intention of traveling to the Indies. The ship did set out but when it stopped at Paimboeuf, Pierre arrived just in time to catch his son and make him promise to travel "only in his imagination". Though this incident is considered exaggerated but it may have been true.

It was during 1840 that Verne wrote one of his earliest prose, *Unprêtreen 1839 (A Priest in 1839)*. By 1847, when Verne was 19, he had taken seriously to writing long works in the style of Victor Hugo, as he wrote two verse tragedies, *Alexandre VI* and *La Conspiration des poudres (The Gunpowder Plot)*. However, his father wanted his son to be an attorney like himself and not a writer.

In 1847, Verne went to Paris to study law. In his second year at the law school, he met Rose Herminie Arnaud Grossetière, a young woman one year his senior, and fell in love with her. He wrote and dedicated thirty poems to the young woman. But her parents disapproved of this match and married her off to someone else. This unfulfilled love affair left a deep impact on the Verne's mind.

Studies in Paris

In July 1848, when Verne left for Paris, he found the city in a political upheaval Due to the French Revolution. Verne entered the city shortly before the election of Louis-Napoléon Bonaparte, who became the first president of the Republic.

Verne used his family connections to enter the Paris society. His uncle Francisque de Châteaubourg introduced him to the literary circle. While continuing his law studies, he fed his passion for the theatre by writing plays. It was also around this time that his health deteriorated and he started suffering from stomach cramps.

In 1851, Verne suffered from the first of the four attacks of facial paralysis. However, the reasons for such attacks remained unknown. The same year, he was spared from enlisting in the French military to his great relief. Though he wrote profusely, he pursued his law studies and graduated with a La Licence de Droit in January 1851.

Literary Debut

Thanks to his visits to salons, Verne came in contact with Alexandre Dumas in 1849. He became close friends with Dumas's son, and also showed him a manuscript for a stage comedy, *Les Paillesrompues* *(The Broken Straws)*. The two young men revised the play and after some arrangements, the play was produced by the Opéra-National at the Théâtre-Historique in Paris, in 1850.

In 1851, Verne met a fellow writer from Nantes, Pierre-Michel-François Chevalier, the editor-in-chief of the magazine *Musée des familles*. Chevalier was looking for reader-friendly articles on geography, history, science and technology—a job perfectly cut out for Verne. He first

offered Chevalier a short historical adventure story, *The First Ships of the Mexican Navy*. It was published followed by *A Voyage in a Balloon*.

After this initial success, Verne entered into a contract with Jules Seveste, a stage director for Théâtre-Historique. Verne became the secretary of the theatre and could now write and produce comic operas. Meanwhile, his father continued to coax him into abandoning writing and starting practice as a lawyer. He even offered Verne to take over his law firm but the latter refused.

Verne then started spending more time at the Bibliothèque Nationale de France, doing research for his stories and feeding his passion for recent discoveries, especially in geography. It was during this period that Verne met the illustrious geographer and explorer Jacques Arago, and with his inspiration, started writing in a new genre called travel writing.

In 1852, two new pieces from Verne appeared in the *Musée des familles*. In April and May 1854, the magazine published Verne's short story *Master Zacharius*. Verne's work for the magazine was cut short in 1856, when he had a serious quarrel with Chevalier and refused to contribute his works to them.

Next, Verne began to formulate a new kind of novel—a novel of science—which would allow him to incorporate large amounts of the factual information. Now with financial stability, Verne married Honorine de Viane, a young widow with two daughters, in 1857. The same year, he published his first book, *Le Salon de 1857 (The 1857 Salon)*.

The Novelist Emerges

In 1859–1860, Verne and his wife took the first of about 20 trips to the British Isles, which inspired Verne to write *Voyage en Angleterre eten Écosse*. In 1861, their only child was born. Soon, his works started getting published. However, it was a meeting with editor and publisher Jules Hetzel that literally turned around Verne's literary career. In 1863, *Five Weeks in a Balloon* was published. The book was widely acclaimed. Verne knew that he had finally found his place in the world. For the next 10 years, he wrote books that went on to become great classics. Around this time, Hetzel introduced Verne to Felix Nadar, who in turn introduced Verne to his circle of scientific friends. These meetings influenced Verne's scientific stories.

Verne Hits His Stride

In 1864, Verne published *Edgar Allan Poe and His Works*, *Adventures of Captain Hatteras* and *Journey to the Center of the Earth*. In 1865, Verne published *From the Earth to the Moon* and *Captain Grant's Children*. He soon bought a ship and with his wife went sailing the seas. His adventures became fodder for his novels. In 1867, Hetzel published Verne's *Geography of France and Her Colonies*. In 1869 and 1870, Hetzel published both volumes of Verne's *Twenty Thousand Leagues under the Sea*, *Round the Moon* and *Discovery of the Earth*. *The Mysterious Island* appeared three years later. By now, Verne's popularity had soared manyfold.

Later Years

Verne got published *The Adventures of a Special Correspondent* (1872), *The Survivors of the Chancellor* (1875), *Michael Strogoff* (1876), and *Dick Sand: A Captain at Fifteen* (1878), among several others. Despite personal tragedies over the next few years, he continued to write. His later works—*Eight Hundred Leagues on the Amazon*, *Robur the Conqueror* and *Master of the World*—were all well received. In 1905, while ill with diabetes, Verne died at his home in Amiens, France.

Legacy

Verne wrote more than 70 books and created numerous memorable characters

and countless innovations years before their time, including the submarine, space travel, terrestrial flight and deep-sea exploration. His works of imagination have appeared in countless forms—from motion pictures to stage, to television. He is often called the "father of science fiction" and is the second most translated writer in the world.

Fast Facts

Known as 'The Father of Science Fiction', Jules Verne is the second most translated author in the world.

LEO TOLSTOY

On September 9, 1828, writer Leo Tolstoy was born at his family's estate, Yasnaya Polyana, in the Tula Province of Russia. He was the youngest of four boys. In 1830, after Tolstoy's mother's death, his father's cousin took over caring for the children. When their father, Count Nikolay Tolstoy, died just seven years later, their aunt was appointed the legal guardian. When the aunt passed away, Tolstoy and his siblings moved in with a second aunt in Kazan, Russia.

Tolstoy received his primary education at home by French and German tutors. In 1843, he enrolled in an Oriental languages programme at the University of Kazan. Since he was not too good at studies, he took up an easier law programme. Prone to partying in excess, Tolstoy ultimately left the university in 1847, without a degree. He returned to his parents' estate, where he tried to be a farmer but remained unsuccessful. He, however, was able to keep his habit of writing journals, a habit that would later inspire him to write his masterpieces.

As Tolstoy was failing on the farm, his elder brother, Nikolay, convinced Tolstoy to join the Army as a junker in the Caucasus Mountains, where he himself was stationed.

Early Publications

While working as a junker for the Army, Tolstoy managed to find enough free time to work on an autobiographical story called *Childhood*. In it, he wrote of his fondest childhood memories. In 1852, Tolstoy submitted the sketch to *The Contemporary*, a popular journal at the time. The story was accepted and became Tolstoy's first published work.

After completing *Childhood*, Tolstoy started writing about his day-to-day life at the Army outpost in the Caucasus.

However, he did not complete the work (*The Cossacks*), until 1862, when he had left the Army. Interestingly, Tolstoy continued to write while at battle during the Crimean War. He wrote *Boyhood* (1854), a sequel to *Childhood*, the second book in what was to become Tolstoy's autobiographical trilogy.

Once the Crimean War had ended and Tolstoy had left the Army, he returned to Russia. Back home, the burgeoning author found himself in high demand. But arrogant and stubborn, he refused to ally himself with any particular intellectual school of thought. Declaring himself an anarchist, he went to Paris in 1857 where he gambled away all his money before returning to Russia. The same year, he got published the third part of his autobiographical trilogy, *Youth*.

In 1862, he produced the first of a 12-issue installment of the journal *Yasnaya Polyana*, and married Sofya Andreyevna Behrs the same year.

Major Novels

Residing at Yasnaya Polyana with his wife and children, Tolstoy spent the better part of the 1860s toiling over his first great novel, *War and Peace*. A portion of the novel was first published in the *Russian Messenger* in 1865, under the title *The Year 1805*. By 1869, the novel was complete. Both critics and the public were buzzing about the novel's historical accounts of the Napoleonic Wars, combined with its thoughtful

development of realistic yet fictional characters. Among the ideas that Tolstoy talks of in *War and Peace* is the belief that the quality and meaning of one's life is mainly derived from one's day-to-day activities.

Following the success of *War and Peace*, in 1873, Tolstoy set to work on the second of his best known novels, *Anna Karenina*. The novel was partially based on current events while Russia was at war with Turkey. Like *War and Peace*, it fictionalized some biographical events from Tolstoy's life. *Anna Karenina* was published in installments from 1873 to 1877, to critical and public acclaim. The success of this book increased his riches.

Religious Conversion

Despite the success of *Anna Karenina*, following the novel's completion, Tolstoy suffered a spiritual crisis. Struggling to uncover the meaning of life, Tolstoy first went to the Russian Orthodox Church, but failed to find the answers he sought. He went on to believe that the Christian churches were corrupt and made their own beliefs. He expressed his thoughts on those beliefs in *The Mediator* in 1883.

Tolstoy courted controversy after the publication and the Russian Orthodox Church ousted him. When Tolstoy's new beliefs prompted his desire to give away his money, his wife strongly objected. Eventually, Tolstoy compromised by conceding to grant his wife the copyrights and the royalties of all his writings predating 1881.

Later Fiction

In addition to his religious tracts, Tolstoy continued to write fiction throughout the 1880s and 1890s. His later works included primarily moral tales and realistic fiction. One of his most successful works during this phase was the novella *The Death of Ivan Ilyich*, written in 1886.

In 1898, Tolstoy wrote *Father Sergius*, a work of fiction in which he criticized the beliefs that he developed following his spiritual conversion. The following year, he wrote his third lengthy novel, *Resurrection*. While the work received some praise, it did not match the acclaim of the previous novels. His later work includes essays on art, a satirical play called *The Living Corpse* and a novella called *Hadji-Murad*, which was published after his death.

Elder Years

Over the last 30 years of his life, Tolstoy established himself as a moral and religious leader. His ideas about non-violent resistance to evil influenced the likes of Mahatma Gandhi. Also during his later years, Tolstoy reaped the rewards of international acclaim. Yet he still struggled to maintain a balance between his religious beliefs and his home. In order to escape the attention that this struggle attracted in the press, Tolstoy along with his youngest daughter, Aleksandra, embarked on a pilgrimage.

Death and Legacy

The pilgrimage undertaken by Tolstoy proved too arduous for the aging novelist. In November 1910, the stationmaster of a train depot in Astapovo, Russia, opened his home to Tolstoy, allowing the ailing writer to rest. Tolstoy died there shortly after, on November 20, 1910. He was buried at the family estate, Yasnaya Polyana, in Tula Province. He was survived by his wife and their brood of 10 children.

To this day, Tolstoy's novels are considered among the finest achievements of literary work. *War

and Peace*, in fact, is frequently cited as the greatest novel ever written. In contemporary academia, Tolstoy is widely acknowledged as having possessed a gift for describing characters' unconscious motives.

Fast Facts

Tolstoy has authored books like War and Peace, Anna Karenina and The Death of Ivan Ilyich, which even today are amongst the world's top literary works.

LEWIS CARROLL

Lewis Carroll was born Charles Lutwidge Dodgson. He was an English logician, mathematician, photographer and novelist. He is well known for his works *Alice's Adventures in Wonderland* and its sequel, *Through the Looking Glass*.

Early Life

Carroll was the eldest son and third child in a family of seven girls and four boys. He was born to Rev. Charles Dodgson and Frances Jane Lutwidge in Daresbury.

The Dodgson children, living in an isolated country village, had few friends.

Young Carroll attended Richmond School, Yorkshire (1844–45), and then proceeded to Rugby School (1846–50). He disliked his four years at public school possibly because he was bullied. He was often ill during this time and one such illness left him deaf in one ear. After attending Rugby, he was home-tutored by his father for a year. He matriculated from Christ Church, Oxford and became an undergraduate at Oxford in 1851.

Carroll excelled in his mathematical and classical studies. As a result, he received studentship and got his Bachelor of Arts degree in December 1854. He was even appointed lecturer in mathematics. Interestingly, he remained unmarried, which was one condition of the studentship at Christ Church. Carroll was ordained a deacon in the Church of England on December 22, 1861.

His association with children grew naturally as he grew up in a large household. All through his life, he suffered from a bad stammer. However, he was able to preach successfully during his later life and, surprisingly, he could speak easily with children. He managed to entertain the three children of Henry George Liddell, dean of Christ Church, too well and they became his friends.

A Writer Emerges

On July 4, 1862, Carroll rowed the three children— Alice Liddell and her sisters Lorina and Edith—up the Thames to Godstow, picnicked on the bank and returned late in the evening. It was during this trip that he told the story of Alice and her adventures to his young companions. Later, as they parted at the door of the deanery, Alice went up to Carroll and said, "Oh, I wish you would write out Alice's adventures for me!" He certainly did write it and even added a few more adventures.

He gave the finished text to Alice Liddell and never gave the story another thought. One day, novelist Henry Kingsley, while visiting the deanery, chanced to read it. He then urged Mrs. Liddell to persuade the author to publish it. On hearing his, Carroll consulted his friend George Macdonald, who read the story to his six year old. His son declared that he "wished there were 60,000 volumes of it."

Accordingly, Carroll revised the text for publication and added more stories to it. He also commissioned a renowned cartoonist to make illustrations for the book. The book was published as *Alice's Adventures in Wonderland* in 1865. *Through the Looking Glass* and *What Alice Found There* came next and were equally popular with readers.

Death and Legacy

Around his 66th birthday, Carroll caught a severe case of influenza, which led to pneumonia. He died on January 14, 1898, leaving an enigma behind him.

By the time of Carroll's death, Alice had become the most popular children's book in England and by 1932, it had perhaps become the most popular book in the world. Besides being a writer, Carroll was also a fine photographer of children and adults. Besides Alice's adventures, Carroll had also written several prose and verse, and a few serious poems. As Charles L. Dodgson, he had written several books on mathematics.

Fast Facts

Carroll's *Alice's Adventures in Wonderland* has been translated into more than 70 languages.

MARK TWAIN

Samuel Langhorne Clemens, who is well known by his pen name, Mark Twain, was born in a small village in Florida, Missouri. He was the sixth child of John and Jane Clemens. When he was four years old, his family moved to Hannibal. Clemens was a storekeeper, lawyer, judge and land speculator. Although he dreamed big, he often found it difficult to make ends meet. Twain's mother, on the other hand, was fun-loving and a tenderhearted homemaker. She told her children stories to while away the winter nights. She became head of the household in 1847 when John died unexpectedly. This was the time when the conditions of the Clemens family further deteriorated.

Twain lived in Hannibal until the age of 17. The town, situated on the Mississippi River, was a splendid place to grow up in. Steamboats arrived there three times a day, tooting their whistles; circuses, minstrel shows and revivalists paid visits; a decent library was available; and tradesmen frequented the town often. However, violence too was common. As a result, Twain saw death quite early in his life.

Life in Hannibal

The town of Hannibal inspired several of Twain's fictional locales, including St. Petersburg in *Tom Sawyer* and *Huckleberry Finn*. These imaginary river towns are complex places: sunlit and exuberant on the one hand, but also vipers' nests of cruelty, poverty, drunkenness and loneliness. Twain had experienced all these at some or the other point in his life.

Twain attended school until he was about

12 years old when, after his father's death, the family had no source of income. It was during this time that Twain found employment as an apprentice printer at the *Hannibal Courier*. He could thus get a meagre ration of food for his family. In 1851, at 15, he secured a job as a printer and occasional writer and editor at the *Hannibal Western Union*, a small newspaper firm.

In 1857, at 21 years of age, Twain fulfilled one of his dreams—that of learning to pilot a steamboat on the Mississippi. He became a licensed pilot by 1859, and in no time, he found regular employment plying the shoals and channels of the great river. His life was exciting, the pay was good and his work had also given him a good status. However, with the outbreak of the Civil War in 1861, his service was cut short as the civilian traffic on the river had come to a halt. He even participated in the war for a few weeks in 1861 before realizing that his future lay in the great American West.

Heading Out West

In July 1861, Twain climbed onboard a stagecoach and headed for Nevada and California, where he would spend the next five years of his life. At first, he prospected for silver and gold but nothing happened. By 1862, he was completely broke and sensed the urgent need for a job.

As Twain knew his way around a newspaper office, he went to work as a

reporter for the *Virginia City Territorial Enterprise*. He churned out news stories, editorials and sketches and it was while being here that he adopted the pen name of Mark Twain, a name he would use for the rest of his life for all his works.

Twain became one of the best-known storytellers in the West. He had a distinctive narrative style, which was friendly, funny, irreverent, often satirical and always eager to deflate the pretentious. He got his first major break in 1865, when one of his tales, *Jim Smiley and His Jumping Frog*, was printed in newspapers and magazines around the country. His next step up the ladder of success came in 1867, when he took a five-month sea cruise in the Mediterranean, writing humorously about the sights for American newspapers with the determination to write a book on the adventures he would have during this trip. He also wrote a book in 1869, *The Innocents Abroad*, which became a bestseller.

At 34, Twain had become one of the most popular and famous writers in America.

Marriage

In those years, the country's cultural life was dictated by an Eastern establishment centred in New York and Boston. All this while, Twain's fervent wish was to get rich, support his mother, rise socially and receive what he called "the respectful regard of a high Eastern civilization."

In February 1870, he married the 24-year-old Olivia Langdon, the daughter of a rich New York coal merchant. She, like many people during that time, took pride in her pious, high-minded, genteel approach to life. Twain hoped that she would "reform" him from his rustic ways. The couple stayed in Buffalo and had four children.

Thankfully, Twain's glorious "low-minded" western voice broke through on occasion. That voice is echoed in the two benchmarks of American literature, *The Adventures of Tom Sawyer* and its sequel *Adventures of Huckleberry Finn*.

Adventures of Huckleberry Finn

"All modern American literature comes from one book by Mark Twain called Huckleberry Finn," wrote Ernest Hemingway in 1935. His comment refers to the language of Twain's masterpiece. It was the first time in America that the vivid, raw, not-so-respectable voice of the common folk was used to create great literature.

Huck Finn was the hard work of many years as Twain often put the work aside. In the meantime, he pursued respectability with the 1881 publication of *The Prince and the Pauper* and later with the publication of *Life on the Mississippi*, in 1883.

From here on, business and writing were of equal value to Twain as he set about his cardinal task of earning money. In 1885, he triumphed as a book publisher by issuing the bestselling memoirs of former President Ulysses S. Grant, who had died recently. He spent many hours on this and other business ventures in the hope of making quick money but instead he soon went bankrupt.

Later Work

Twain's financial failings, in some ways like his father's, left a deep impact on his mind and he became a pessimist. Another cause of his angst, perhaps, was his unconscious anger at himself for not giving undivided attention to his deepest creative instincts, which centred on his Missouri boyhood.

In 1889, Twain published *A Connecticut Yankee in King Arthur's Court*, a science-fiction/historical novel about ancient England. His next major work was *The Tragedy of Pudd'nhead Wilson*. He continued to write short stories, essays and several other books, including a study of Joan of Arc. *The Chronicle of Young Satan*, his unfinished work at the time of his death, is greatly admired today.

Twain's last 15 years were filled with public honours, including degrees from Oxford and Yale, and lots of travel.

Personal Struggles

The later years of his life were replete with anguish and heartbreaks. Early in their marriage, he and Livy had lost their toddler son; in 1896, his daughter, Susy, died at 24. This tragedy broke his heart. Next, his youngest daughter was diagnosed with severe epilepsy. In 1909, she died of a heart attack at 29. For several years, Twain's relationship with his middle daughter Clara remained strained. In June 1904, while Twain was travelling, Livy died after a prolonged illness.

Twain became somewhat bitter in his later years, even while projecting an amiable persona to the public. In private, he demonstrated a stunning insensitivity to friends and loved ones. During his last years, he wrote fervently but his memory faltered. He died on April 21, 1910, at the age of 74, at his country home in Redding, Connecticut.

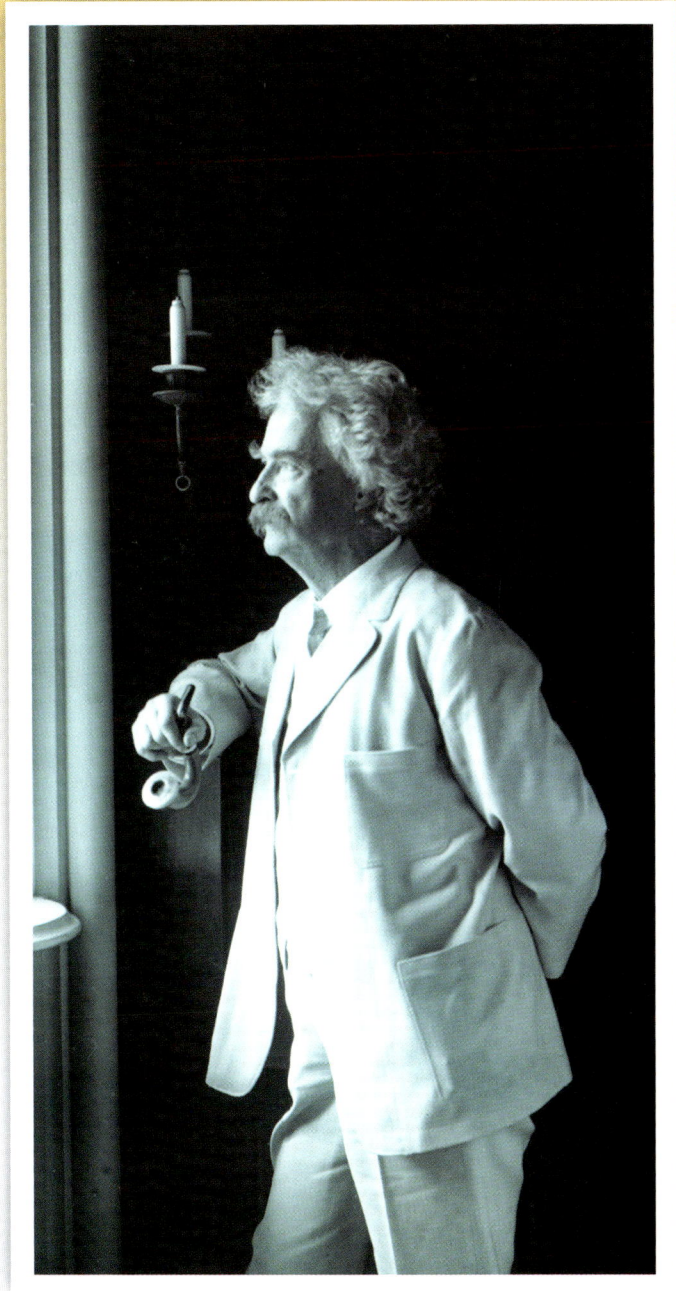

Fast Facts

In 1976, an asteroid was named for Mark Twain: 2362 Mark Twain.

RABINDRANATH TAGORE

Rabindranath Tagore was a Bengali poet, novelist and painter. He became the first non-European to be awarded the Nobel Prize for Literature in 1913 for his book *Gitanjali, Song Offerings*. Tagore played a key role in introducing Indian culture to the West and is generally regarded as an outstanding creative artist of modern India. W.B Yeats and André Gide have greatly praised his work. Only a small fraction of Tagore's work has been translated into other languages. He himself had translated many of his works.

Early Years

Tagore was born in Jorasanko (Tagore House) in Kolkata, India. He was the fourteenth child born to Debendranath Tagore and Sarada Devi. His grandfather, Dwarkanath Tagore, was a social reformer and a wealthy landowner. Tagore grew up in a progressive family, where numerous social and cultural events took place. Often theatrical and musical performances were staged in their mansion. Debendranath travelled widely during his career and was a proponent of the Brahmo Samaj, a social and religious movement also known as the Bengal Renaissance. Years later, his son Rabindranath too would follow in his footsteps.

Although there were times spent swimming in the Ganges River and hiking, Tagore's childhood days were mostly confined to the family estate under the watchful eye of the servants. He was mostly home tutored as he did not do well at school. At home, he studied a wide array of subjects including; art, history, science, mathematics, Bengali, Sanskrit and English, Hindu scriptures, romantic poetry like that of Percy Bysshe Shelley and classical poetry, notably of Kalidasa. As his father travelled frequently, Tagore could rarely spend time with him. When Tagore was 13, his mother passed away.

Early Writings

Tagore started writing poetry from an early age. Some of his poems were published anonymously or under his pen name 'Bhanusingha' [Sun Lion]. Soon, he became a regular contributor to magazines like *Balaka* and *Bharati*. His first collection, *Kabi Kahini (Tale of a Poet)*, was published in 1878. He also started writing short stories including his first: *Bhikharini* (1877) (The Beggar Woman).

Tagore had travelled across many countries in his life. However, his first trip was with his father when he was 13. During this trip, he travelled across the breadth of the country. A few years later, he went to England to attend the University College in London from 1878–1880. At that time he had wanted to be a barrister. But he never finished his studies. During this time, he wrote one of his most famous poems: *Nirjharer Swapnabhanga (The Fountain Awakened from its Dream)*.

At the age of 22, in 1883, Tagore married Bhabatarini (later known as Mrinalini) Devi. Together, they had five children. In 1890, Tagore moved to the vast family estate in Shilaidaha, which is now in Bangladesh. His wife and children joined him in 1898. He collected taxes from the villagers on a barge. It was during these times that he observed the village life and learnt the ways of the villagers. He was charmed by their pastoral life working in the rice fields, watching the fishermen with their nets, visiting school children and attending feasts that were held in his honour. His experiences in the pastoral life became fodder for many of his works. During his stay at Shilaidaha, he wrote prolifically and completed prestigious works like *Chitra: A Play in One Act*, *Manasi* (poetry) [The Ideal One], and *Sonar Tari* [Golden Boat].

Shantiniketan

The next period of Tagore's life involved his founding of the school in Shantiniketan. Established in 1901, the school today is known as Visva-Bharati University. The school was an experiment done by Tagore for he had based his school and his method of education on the ashrama model with pioneering emphasis on learning in a harmonious and natural setting. He felt that an education based on understanding the environment by using one's five senses was a better way to teach children. The education system is now a prestigious open air university and a universal meeting place for the East and the West.

Tagore's wife died just one year after he had founded the university. He remembered his wife by writing poems in *Smaran (In Memoriam)*. Other works written or published during this period were *Katha O Kahini (Tales and Stories)*, *Naivedya*, *Kheya*, *Raja (The King of the Dark Chamber)*, *Dak-Ghar (The Post Office)*, *The Crescent Moon*, *Gitimalya (Wreath of Songs)*, *Songs of Kabîr*, *Stray Birds*, *Sadhana: The Realisation of Life*, and *Balaka (The Flight of Cranes)*, and the poems *Fruit-Gathering*, *The Fugitive* and *The Gardener*.

Tagore's novel *Ghare-Baire* (1915) (*The Home and the World*) and *Glimpses of Bengal: Selected from the Letters of Sir Rabindranath Tagore* (1885–1895) were published in 1920.

Travels and Acclaim

In time, Tagore travelled to the United States and England to speak of his work at Shantiniketan. He also brought with him some English translations of his poems from *Gitanjali*. His poems were soon read by many fellow authors including Ezra Pound, Ernest Rhys and Yeats. It was a matter of time before he earned his Nobel Prize for Literature in 1913 because of his profoundly sensitive, fresh and beautiful verse. An introduction to *Gitanjali* was written by Nobel Prize winning poet W.B. Yeats. Some of the poems are written in colloquial language and they revolve around the themes of naturalism, mysticism and philosophical insight. Post *Gitanjali*, Tagore was invited to many North American and European cities, where he gave long lectures and did readings. On his trips, he also met other illustrious figures of the day including Albert Einstein, Robert Frost, Thomas Mann, H.G. Wells and Mahatma Gandhi. In 1915, he was made a knight by the British crown but he renounced it in 1919 as he condemned the Jallianwala Bagh Massacre where hundreds of innocent people were killed by soldiers of the British Indian Army.

Hall of Fame

Rabindranath Tagore
Poet, Novelist, Painter

Mark Twain
Writer, Lecturer

Lewis Carroll
Writer, Mathematician
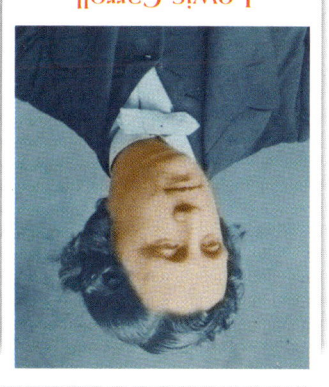

Leo Tolstoy
Novelist, Essayist

Jules Verne
Novelist, Playwright
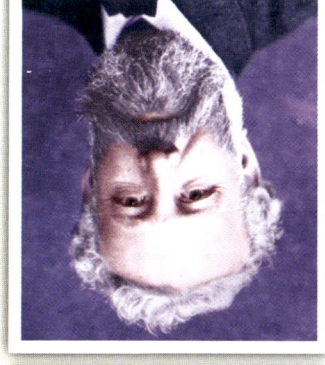

William Shakespeare
Playwright, Poet, Actor

J.R.R. Tolkien
Novelist, Academic
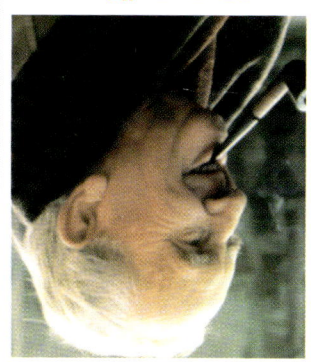

Charles Dickens
Novelist

Jane Austen
Novelist

Alexandre Dumas
Playwright, Novelist

J.K. Rowling
Novelist

Arthur Conan Doyle
Novelist, Physician

48

the twists and turns of Shakespeare's plots, destroying the hero and those whom he loves.

In Shakespeare's final period, he wrote several tragicomedies. Among these are *Cymbeline*, *The Winter's Tale* and *The Tempest*. Though graver in tone than the comedies he wrote, they are not the dark tragedies in the likes of *King Lear* or *Macbeth* simply because his later plays end with forgiveness for the crimes committed and in reconciliation.

Death

Tradition has it that Shakespeare died on his birthday, though this is not true. On the other hand, church records show that he was interred at Trinity Church on April 25, 1616.

Today, his plays remain highly popular and are constantly studied and reinterpreted in performances with diverse cultural and political contexts. The genius of Shakespeare's characters and plots is that they portray human emotions and their complexity, and the circumstances that people find themselves in.

Fast Facts

Apart from writing his numerous plays and sonnets, Shakespeare was also an actor who performed many of his own plays as well as those of other playwrights.

Shakespeare primarily used a metrical pattern consisting of lines of unrhymed iambic pentameter or blank verse to compose his plays. At the same time, there are passages in all the plays that deviate from this and use forms of poetry or simple prose.

Early Works: Histories and Comedies

With the exception of Romeo and Juliet, Shakespeare's first plays were mostly histories written in the early 1590s. Richard II, Henry VI (parts 1, 2 and 3) and Henry V dramatize the destructive results of weak or corrupt rulers.

Shakespeare also wrote several comedies during his early period: A Midsummer Night's Dream, The Merchant of Venice, Much Ado About Nothing, As You Like It and Twelfth Night. Other plays, possibly written before 1600, include Titus Andronicus, The Comedy of Errors, The Taming of the Shrew and The Two Gentlemen of Verona.

Later Works: Tragedies and Tragicomedies

It was in Shakespeare's later period, after 1600, that he wrote the tragedies Hamlet, King Lear, Othello and Macbeth. In these, Shakespeare's characters present vivid impressions of human temperament that are timeless and universal. Possibly the best known of these plays is Hamlet, which explores betrayal, retribution, incest and moral failure. These moral failures often drive

admired by people of high rank. Despite this, the artists had many nobles acting as patrons of the performing arts and actors. Early in his career, Shakespeare was able to attract the attention of Henry Wriothesley, the Earl of Southampton, to whom he dedicated his first and second published poems: Venus and Adonis (1593) and The Rape of Lucrece (1594).

Establishing Himself

By 1597, as many as 15 out of 37 plays written by Shakespeare had been published. During this time, it is recorded that he spent most of his time in London writing and once a year came home during the 40-day Lenten period, when the theatres were closed.

By 1599, Shakespeare and his business partners had built their own theatre on the south bank of the Thames River. They named the theatre, The Globe. In 1605, Shakespeare purchased leases of real estate near Stratford for £ 440, which doubled in value and earned him £ 60 a year. This made him an entrepreneur as well as an artist.

Writing Style

Shakespeare wrote his early plays in the conventional style with elaborate metaphors and rhetorical phrases. He, however, soon invented his own distinct style making his writings innovative and with a freer flow of words. With only small degrees of variation, led some to raise questions about the authorship of his work.

Married Life

William Shakespeare was just 18 when he married 26-year-old Anne Hathaway on November 28, 1582, in Worcester, Canterbury Province. Their first child, a daughter they named Susanna, was born on May 26, 1583. Two years later, on February 2, 1585, twins Hamnet and Judith were born.

After the birth of the twins, there are seven years of William Shakespeare's life where no records exist. There is speculation as to what Shakespeare did during these 'lost years'. One theory is that he might have gone into hiding for poaching game from the local landlord, Sir Thomas Lucy. Another possibility is that he might have been working as an assistant schoolmaster in Lancashire. It is generally believed that he arrived in London in the mid to late 1580s and that he may have found work as a horse attendant at some of London's finer theatres.

Theatrical Beginnings

By 1592, there is evidence of Shakespeare earning a living as an actor and a playwright in London and also of producing several plays. The September 20, 1592 edition of the Stationers' Register includes an article by London playwright Robert Greene that takes a few jabs at Shakespeare.

Scholars however agree on the fact that perhaps Shakespeare was trying to reach above his rank by matching the skills of renowned playwrights like Christopher Marlowe, Thomas Nashe and Greene. By the early 1590s, documents reveal that Shakespeare was a managing partner in the Lord Chamberlain's Men, an acting company in London. After the crowning of King James I in 1603, the company changed its name to the King's Men. The company was famous and records show that many of Shakespeare's plays were published and were sold as popular literature. The theatre culture in 16th century England was not highly

45

WILLIAM SHAKESPEARE

William Shakespeare is perhaps the most notable name in the world of English literature. For the last 400 years, Shakespeare's plays have been performed in countless hamlets, villages, cities and metropolises and yet, there are several mysteries surrounding the life of the bard from Avon. There are two primary sources that provide historians with a basic outline of his life. The first is his work—the plays, poems and sonnets—while the second include documents that available in church and in court records. However, these two sources combined only manage to give us a modest glimpse of the life of William Shakespeare.

Early Life

Though no birth records exist, church records indicate that a William Shakespeare was baptized at Holy Trinity Church in Stratford-upon-Avon on April 26, 1564. From this, scholars assume that Shakespeare was born around this date and usually April 23, 1564 is taken to be his birth date.

Located 103 miles west of London, during Shakespeare's time Stratford-upon-Avon was a market-town bisected with a country road and the River Avon. He was the third child of John Shakespeare, a leather merchant, and Mary Arden, a local landed heiress. He had two elder sisters and three younger brothers. His father was a successful merchant and had held official positions as alderman and bailiff.

Nothing is known about the childhood of Shakespeare or where he had completed his education. Only estimations are made about his education at school. Some scholars even conclude that he may have been home tutored as his father was a man of influence. At the same time, the uncertainty regarding his education has

Later Years

In 1921, Tagore and agricultural economist Leonard Elmhirst founded the Institute for Rural Reconstruction, 'Shriniketan' (Abode of Peace), near Shantiniketan. He continued to travel and write despite his preoccupation with his organizations. In 1937, he was stricken by a lengthy illness, becoming comatose at times. He never fully recovered from his illness. He however continued to write. Some say that he had written his finest work during the last 5 years of his life. Tagore died on August 7, 1941, at the family estate Jorasanko, where he was born.

Legacy

Tagore was a humanitarian and a social and religious reformer. He was caught up between the cultures that the British brought and that which he grew up in. He was a patriot and he composed the national anthem when India gained independence. Another of his poems was chosen as Bangladesh's national anthem. Tagore was a polymath and he is fondly remembered for composing hundreds of beautiful poems and songs. His poems and songs are called Rabindra sangeet. He has also produced a wide collection of paintings and drawings along with various dramas, novels, essays, operas, short stories, travel diaries, correspondence and autobiographies.

Fast Facts

Rabindranath Tagore is the only poet to have composed national anthems for two nations—India and Bangladesh.